Copyright © 2013 by Michael Synk

All rights reserved. No part of this book my be reproduced or transmitted in any form or by any means, electronic or mechanical, including photocopying, recording, or by any information storage and retrieval system, without permission from the publisher.

In-Synk: Aligning Strategy, Actions and Goals
1610 E. Clanlo Drive
Memphis, TN 38014

www.in-synk.com

Cover Design by Tactical Magic

Layout Design by Andi Crawford-Andrus

ROCK & SAND

A Practical Insight to Business Growth

by Michael Synk

IN-SYNK

Aligning Strategies, Actions and Goals

www.rocknsand.net

CONTENTS

TESTIMONIALS

"Strategic planning is exciting and sexy. Deciding what comes next and then executing it is confusing and difficult. Rock and Sand takes the mystery out of these critical steps. This model is clear and compelling. It's a practical and straightforward insight that will move your organization forward. Michael Synk has moved an important rock for all of us."

   –Verne Harnish, Author of "Mastering the Rockefeller Habits, Creator of The One Page Strategic Plan™", Founder of Gazelles, Inc.

"Effective business leaders must know the answers to two fundamental questions that drive profitable growth: "What is our strategy?" and "How will we make that happen?" Both are regularly overcomplicated beyond practicality by authors, experts, and consultants with a stake in promoting strategy as a complicated enterprise. Michael Synk has created a straightforward, simple model that not only debunks the complexity myth, but also facilitates execution – getting things done – as an integral component of good strategy. If you're serious about growing your business and if you're a fan of simplicity over complexity – this is the book for you."

   –Mark Green, President, Performance Dynamics Group, LLC

"Have you ever wondered about the analogy of moving 'rocks' during your Gazelles training session? I have always found it a peculiar analog. Where are we moving them? I imagined my team lugging big rocks down a field on a hot day and measuring success as an end zone. Michael's explanation and visualization is something that fits the world view of my team and I. As a team we push sand and can always do that bigger, faster, or stronger. We all know that's not strategic but easy to point to as progress. Strategic growth occurs when my team gets behind a big rock and we push hard and collectively to fill in big gaping holes in our business. It is the sustainable foundation of both rocks and sand on which all businesses need to stand."

—Eric Mathews, Founder and CEO of LaunchYourCity, Inc, a venture development organization and startup ecosystem builder in the Southeastern United States.

FOREWORD

I have known Michael Synk as a certified Gazelles Coach, colleague and friend for over a decade, and consider him to be one of the people who best communicate the elegantly simple Gazelles One-Page Planning and 4 Decisions Processes in the most compelling and easy-to-understand ways.

When he shared with me a preview of his "Rock and Sand" Model a few weeks ago, and having since that time also watched his short Video and read the full manuscript for his new book, I quickly concluded that Michael had done it again – this time taken a simple concept for developing and communicating Strategy, and made it even more simple and understandable for more people to enjoy and deploy.

The Model really comes down to one of our fundamental Gazelles Growth Company principles: If you're not moving, and not moving something meaningful, each and every month, quarter and year, you are standing still – or worse, you are falling further and further behind your competition. No way to run a Fast Growth Company!

Michael's "Rock and Sand" Model helps you make the crucial Strategic decisions that allow you to identify and select the Right Rocks for you and your business or organization during any given timeframe – whether the next 3-5 years, the next year, the next 90 days, or the next month.

On the Strategic level, he gives you the Big Five Strategy Questions that will quickly help you pinpoint opportunities to lock in significant strategic advantages for you and your business. Give Michael's "Rock and Sand" Model a quick read, view his Video, and you will be doing yourself and your company a HUGE favor, while reaping the benefits of sound and disciplined Strategic Thinking and Decision Making!

–Ron Huntington, Founder, Past President,
  Head Coach Emeritus of Gazelles International Coaches.

CHAPTER 1

STRATEGY IS EVERYWHERE

Strategy comes in all shapes and sizes to fit all sorts of organizations, from enormous to tiny. It fits all markets, segments, industries, personalities, income levels, nations, states, counties, cities and neighborhoods.

Of course, books about strategy abound. A simple search on a leading online bookseller done in March 2013 of "Business Strategy " pulls up a whopping list of 84,917 titles. As you read this, rest assured there are more added to the list each month. You've heard the litany of titles: *Blue Ocean Strategy; Big Think Strategy; Good Strategy, Bad Strategy; Strategic DNA; Strategic Planning for Dummies, The Lords of Strategy, The Art of Strategy, Thinking Strategically, The Strategist, The Strategy Focused Organization*….and so on. Multiple books on strategy have been written by Porter, Peters, Hamel, Pralahad, Collins, Deming, and Drucker. Every professor of strategy trying to achieve tenure has written one as well. Don't forget that the titans of industry have to write them too. Jack Welch has written three and there is one from every one of his lieutenants who left the fold to make his fortune elsewhere. The genre has been around a long time, starting with Sun Tzu's *The Art of War*.

Are you getting the picture? There is no of lack of guidance about strategy.

I've read many of these books, and I've put much of what I've learned from them to work with my clients. There are lots of ways to develop good strategy. Having different ways to look at strategy can be enlightening, stimulating the creative thought that creates the best plans.

Yet within this vast library of books on strategy, something is missing. Concrete models for execution are largely absent from the material. Execution is almost entirely left up to the reader.

But don't think that "Business Execution" books don't exist either. A similar search on the same national online bookseller lists 5106 "Busines Execution" titles, a much smaller number. I've read a number of these books as well, and most are worthwhile. But, of the ones I've read, none of them tie execution back to strategy.

This is a gross oversimplification, but all the execution literature seems to be progressions of the priority and time management principles outlined originally by Ben Franklin in his Autobiography, only expanded to fit teams and organizations. They articulate important leadership tactics for getting things done faster, better and with less energy. Yet, like the strategy books, tying these important habits back to strategy is left up to the reader.

This "missing link" between strategy and execution is a problem. Good strategies are developed but don't get executed. Great execution habits are learned and applied to actions that end up leading organizations to places they don't want to go. Very quickly, strategy and execution turns into doing what was already being done, only now with an emphasis on doing it faster and better, and trying harder.

These types of strategy and execution are one dimensional. "More is better, let's do more." It's rigid. It's tedious. It's expensive.

Growth can be steady, yet it is hardly exponential. When significant growth occurs, it is a function of serendipity, not intent. It's "strategy after the fact," back filled from results.

Yet this is where the vast majority of businesses live, strategically and on execution.

We need a way to think and speak about strategy and execution that is simple, productive, and definitive while building a bridge between strategy and execution. It needs it to be fundamentally sound and motivation-ally inspiring, so that alignment and linkage between strategy and execution occurs.

We don't need another strategy or execution book. We need a book that spans the gap between the two. That's what this book is about.

As with most things worth thinking, talking, and writing about, it comes down to asking the right question.

Here it is.

Are you "pushing sand" or "moving rocks?"

CHAPTER 2

ARE YOU "PUSHING SAND" OR "MOVING ROCKS?"

You're "pushing sand" when you are performing the basic tasks of your business. A comprehensive list of these activities includes the following: advertising, sales, taking orders, making product, delivering service, billing, and collecting. In short, these are the activities that must be done to transact business. Do them poorly, the sand slips between your fingers, and you lose money. Do them well and you make money. "Pushing sand" is pretty basic concept. You have to do it well to stay in business.

You're "moving rocks" when you are working on something that makes "pushing the sand" easier, faster, or more profitable. When "moving a rock," you might be adding a product line, or you might be improving a production process. You could be expanding your territory, or you could be expanding your technology. It could be a new sales campaign, a new marketing campaign, or a new safety campaign. It could be as simple as adding one especially well qualified employee, or as complicated as adding a whole new department. Sometimes it's not about adding but subtracting: narrowing your focus, narrowing your offerings, and eliminating steps and waste. But whatever the rock, moving it makes it easier to push more sand, faster, and more profitably.

There are three scenarios you might find yourself in:

1. You are pushing sand, but not moving rocks. If you are successful at pushing the sand, you are surviving, but only until someone figures out how to do it better than you. You aren't really growing.

2. You are moving rocks, but not pushing sand. You are still proving your business model. You don't have cash flow. You've got to find and push some sand before you can say you are growing.

3. You are pushing sand successfully and moving rocks productively. You are finding ways to push more and more sand. Your business is quite likely growing.

Which of the three scenarios would you prefer to find yourself in?

CHAPTER 3

THE ROCK AND SAND MODEL

Let's visualize this model.

This is an easy analogy. Imagine that the current status of your company is the middle of a deep hole, something like a mineshaft or well in which you are working your way up to the top from the bottom. Your current status is where you are right now. Where you want to be in three to five years is your long term goal. You want to get from where you are right now to where you will be the future. This is what it looks like:

On one side of the hole there is a pile of sand: a big pile of sand which represents the basic tasks of your company that you do to transact business. Completing these activities equates to pushing sand into the hole. The more tasks you complete the more sand you are pushing into the hole. The sand piles up in the hole and your company gets a bit closer to the top of the hole. It looks something like this:

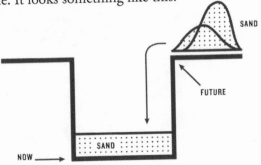

Pushing sand takes a lot of time and effort. It's painstaking at the least and exhaustive at its worst. It moves your company rather slowly towards the top of the hole. To push greater amounts of sand into the hole requires equal increases in both time and effort. The return on effort is costly.

On the other side of the hole is a pile of big rocks. Each one represents a different new initiative that, if completed, could make it easier for you to push more sand or get more value for the sand you are already pushing. When you complete one of these initiatives, you are moving a rock into the hole. It takes up space and allows the sand to pile up faster, moving your company to the top of the hole faster than before. It looks like this:

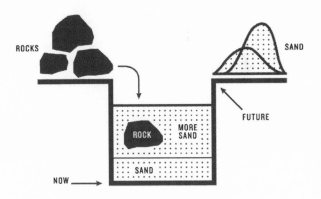

Over time, you keep pushing sand and moving rocks; pushing sand to transact business and moving rocks so you can transact business more easily, faster and for a bigger return. When done successfully, you reach your goal more quickly, in affect getting to the top of the hole faster.

Go to www.RocknSand.net to view a video illustration of this chapter.

CHAPTER 4

NO ROCKS, NO GROWTH

It comes down to this: if your company isn't moving rocks, it isn't growing.

Think about it in terms of our analogy. While sand may be easy to work with, it's hardly a foundation for growth. Sand is almost fluid, isn't it? It shifts with the wind. It melts into mud with the addition of water. It can dissipate instantaneously.

The sand your enterprise is pushing into its hole can change just as quickly. Markets change, competitors appear, technologies evolve, the economy shifts. Your sand pile can literally disappear overnight.

Rocks, on the other hand, are more formidable. They take up space. They have size and weight. They can fit together and have a multiplier effect on each other. They have substance. Moving them, albeit difficult, makes a difference and changes the lay of the land.

Moving rocks changes the landscape as well, only this time to your benefit. Consider the following rocks:

- A new product line helps you to push more sand to your existing customers. Or maybe it adds a disappear as the sand pile shifts, gets blown away or just plain runs out. You have to move rocks to achieve sustainable growth. whole new set of customers.

- New talent brought into the company helps you see better ways to push the sand.

- A technology upgrade can make the pushing of sand more efficient.

- Fresh market research helps you find more piles of sand that you can push from new markets.

- A new or improved process lets you deploy resources to other opportunities. In each case the trajectory of the business changes.

If you aren't working on a rock your business is at best standing still and at worst moving backward. Even if your sand pile is big and your results look good on paper, your business is not growing. The results are illusory and will disappear as the sand pile shifts, gets blown away or just plain runs out.

You have to move rocks to achieve sustainable growth.

CHAPTER 5

WHICH ROCK IS THE RIGHT ONE?

So which rock do you push?

It's a difficult question.

There are a lot of potential rocks to move and with so many to choose from, the decision to focus on just one can be paralyzing in and of itself. Here are some rules for figuring this out.

<u>Never, ever, try to move more than one or two rocks at one time.</u> Trying to move more dilutes your efforts and resources. Let's say you have determined that you have 5 rocks you think you need to move this year. And, as I have often witnessed, you enlist a team to take responsibility for each one. Remember that these teams are full of individuals who are also working hard to push sand, which is their primary responsibility. Each rock gets moved a little bit, but not all the way into the hole, resulting in incremental improvements in a number of areas, but no real impact that makes a significant difference and delivers growth. Instead limit yourself to one rock, or at most two, and align the entire team around moving the rock. More people giving more effort in a concentrated and collaborative manner gets the job done.

<u>Don't select a "me too," rock.</u> By this I mean don't pick a rock just because a competitor or other companies are working on something similar. "Following the herd" is rarely a good move. Make sure there are other reasons for your selection, reasons that are truly relevant to your situation. Don't be lured by the shiny rocks that exist, either. Pay attention to

the trends to avoid trendiness. Select a few of these "me too" rocks in a row and you will wear your team out without much result.

Think about the rock that will have the "biggest impact" or make the "biggest difference." What's the biggest problem to be solved or the biggest opportunity to capitalize on? Is there a rock you can move that significantly closes the gap on a problem or eliminates it? Is there a rock you can move that will help you exploit the opportunity faster or better or more profitably? Is there a rock you can move that changes the game entirely? Think through these questions thoroughly and determine which rock in your pile fits this one of these scenarios. Quantify and qualify and make a selection. And then set it aside for a moment to address the dilemma outlined in the next paragraph.

Does another rock come first? Often you and your team aren't ready to move the biggest and most important rock. Something else comes first. Maybe you don't have the talent, maybe you don't have the knowledge, or the cash, or the technology. Maybe you have to learn how to work together first. Maybe something has to be put in place or removed to be able to get to the rock. Maybe the big all important rock is too big to move right now and you have to move a few to be ready to move the important one.

What's the calendar look like? This last question is helpful to work through when determining time frames for each rock. Some rocks are best moved during certain times of the year as opposed to others. Maybe you have a busy season, where the rock for that particular period can't be anything else except "getting through the busy season" as productively as possible. Maybe there is a special event or two or three on your calendar, such as important trade shows or conferences that can't be ignored and must be worked through.

Think through and argue through each one of these rules, select a rock and commit to it.

CHAPTER 6

THE BIG 5 STRATEGY QUESTIONS

The previous section outlines a process for determining which rock is the right one. It works pretty well. But if you start the process after answering the Big Five Strategy Questions, it works even better.

Consider these Big Five Strategy Questions?

1. <u>Why do we exist?</u> – The answer to this question gives your company both meaning and purpose. It is often referred to by strategy experts as the <u>Purpose Statement</u> or <u>Mission Statement.</u> It should be simple and clear. It expresses what is at the heart of the business. It adds noble purpose and aspiration to the enterprise.

2. <u>How should we behave?</u> – The answers to these questions are the DNA of the company. They convey to the team what is desired behavior and what isn't. Strategy experts refer to these as <u>Core Values</u>. They go beyond simple "permission to play" values such as honesty and integrity. They express the spirit of team, the tone of behavior, and the ethical pillars of the company.

3. <u>What are we good at?</u> – Often referred to as <u>Core Competencies</u>, these answers tell you where to begin and what to build on. These are the processes and procedures you are the best at, or can get better at than anyone else in your market or industry. It's the starting point of strategy; it's the strengths of your company that you build on or add to in order to grow.

4. <u>Where do we want to end up?</u> – Every company needs a sense of direction in order to grow. This is the long term

outcome for the company. It's often referred to as the Vision. Jim Collins calls it the <u>Big Hairy Audacious Goal</u> (BHAG). It's where you are going and where you want to end up at least ten years down the road.

5. <u>Why should customers do business with us?</u> – Is there a compelling reason for customers to buy from you or use your service? It usually isn't price. It needs to be customer-driven not company-driven. It addresses the needs of your key customers and expands from there to other customer groups. It is often referred to as the <u>Brand Promise</u>, or <u>Value Proposition</u>.

When you answer these questions, write them down, and use them by actively and regularly sharing them with your team. Your Big Five Answers become guardrails for all of the decisions about growth for your team, keeping the company moving down the highway and out of the ditches that line the road. Most importantly they create the context for the process of selecting the right rock.

Context is king when selecting a rock. There are lots of ways determine and codify the answers to these questions. Being a Gazelles Certified Coach, I recommend the One Page Strategic Plan™, the Four Decisions™ Model, and *Mastering the Rockefeller Habits* by Verne Harnish. But other methodologies work as well. It's not about the form or format. It's about facilitating deep dialogue within your company, supported by data, that uncovers the answers to the Big Five Strategy Questions.

CHAPTER 7
DO THE NUMBERS:
3 YEARS > 1 YEAR > NEXT 90 DAYS

After defining your Big Five Strategy Answers, it's time to look forward and predict the future for your business. Set some specific outcomes for your business, some milestones to hit somewhere down the road.

Use your Big Five Strategy Answers to guide you through a game of "Let's Pretend" Pick a year, between 3 and five years out and "pretend" that you have been relatively successful at living the Big Five Strategy Answers. Envision your team is living the Core Values, your team is building their Core Competencies and leveraging them to deliver on your Brand Promise. Extrapolate from this scenario and conceptualize the positive results your company has achieved. "Pretend" that all of it is happening because the team is sticking to the Purpose or Mission of the company. And finally, "pretend" you have moved closer to reaching your BHAG.

Extend the game of "Let's Pretend" and decide what numbers you have to hit 3-5 years out: Revenue, expenses, net profit, cash flow, market share, # of customers, revenue per employee. Do the same for any industry specific numbers you measure or track.

Work backwards from your 3-5 year projection and decide what numbers you have to hit in the coming year to be able to hit your 3-5 year numbers.

Work backwards from one year and set the numbers you have to hit in the next 90 days to be able to hit your one year numbers.

Play this game of "Let's Pretend" in pencil. Keep playing with the numbers until you are comfortable with them. They should be realistic, but also ambitious: difficult to achieve if all you do is continue to push the sand, but easier to accomplish if you figure out the right rocks to move that makes them attainable.

CHAPTER 8

THRUSTS > INITIATIVES > ROCKS

The game of "Let's Pretend" continues. Once again you'll be working backwards from three years to one year to the next 90 days. Knowing and accepting the numbers that you need to hit for 3 years, ask and then answer the following questions:

1. What capabilities or competencies are missing that we need to have in place in next three years to hit the 3 year projections?

2. What do have to get better at or learn in the next three years to hit the numbers?

3. What departments/technologies/people do we need to add in the next three years to hit the numbers?

The answers to these questions will be the <u>Key Thrusts</u> of your company for the next 3 years. Don't worry too much about how you will execute them right now. Just decide on them and commit to them.

Continue the "Let's Pretend" game with the one year time frame. Knowing that you have to hit the one year numbers and that to hit the 3 year numbers you have to make progress on the Key Thrusts, ask and then answer this question:

Breaking down the key thrusts into parts, what 3-5 rocks should I move this year that will move the company forward?

When answering this question keep two things in mind. First, while you are moving these rocks during the next year, the team has to keep pushing sand, so don't bite off more than you can chew. Second, be cognizant of the resources you have available to assign to these rocks. An additional rock might be shifting people or adding a person to be able move one of the rocks. This might become a rock in and of itself.

The rocks you decide to move on in the coming year are your **Initiatives**. Finally, extend the game of "Let's Pretend" to the next 90 days. There is only one question to answer at this point.

Which one or two of these rocks should we move right now? (review section 5) These are your <u>Rocks</u>.

Again, keep in mind that in the next ninety days, while you are moving the selected Rock, your company has to continue pushing sand.

CHAPTER 9

THE LITTLE 3 EXECUTION QUESTIONS

Now you have a rock and you need to move it. It's time to apply the Little Three Execution Questions.

Who? What? When?

From a big picture point of view you have already answered two of the questions: "What" is the rock and the "When" is ninety days from now. The "Who" is the person who is responsible for making sure the rock gets moved successfully. Responsibility has to be assigned to one and only one person. Others can be assigned to the team that moves the rock and can be assigned accountability for certain parts of the rock, but only one person can be responsible. When multiple people are responsible for one thing, no one is responsible.

You aren't done with the Little Three Execution Questions yet. The "Who" that has taken responsible for the rock needs to take "Who, What, and When" to the entire team he will be working with to move the rock. The team should create a to do list on all the items that need to be completed in the process of moving the rock, then for each particular "task" the leader needs to ask "What will be done?" "Who will do it?" and "When it will be completed"

At least weekly, review this "Who, What, When" list. Check off what is accomplished; figure out how to check off the ones that are stalled. List new items to be added to the list as you move forward, adding the "Who" and the "When" until your list is complete. Keep this rhythm going until your the rock is completely moved into the hole.

The Little Three Execution Questions just might be more powerful than the Big Five Strategy Questions. They are about getting things done. They keep commitments front and center and help you measure progress. They keep the team engaged and moving forward, which in turn moves your company forward.

Shouldn't you be using "Who, What, When" on every actionable item in your company?

CHAPTER 10
WHAT ABOUT THE SAND?

Don't ever forget about the sand.

When everyone is excited and working hard at moving a rock, it's easy to forget about the sand. Don't ever let this happen. If you do, you are putting your company at risk. You'll run out of the cash you need to move the rocks. Rocks don't fund your company, the sand does. Pushing sand creates the revenue and then the profits that become the cash that pays for the resources needed to move your rock. If you don't keep pushing the sand, you won't be moving any rocks for very much longer. Your business will be shrinking instead of growing.

It's not a case of choosing to move the rock <u>OR</u> to push the sand. It's a case of choosing to move the rock <u>AND</u> to push the sand. You have to do both at the same time.

While choosing your rock for the quarter, and committing the proper resources to moving it, the same attention is to be applied to the sand. In effect, give the sand equal status to a rock. Commit to pushing it and commit to succeeding at it. Use the Little Three Execution Questions to do this.

- Assign responsibility and accountability for each part of pushing the sand. (Who)

- Determine the activities that push the sand and measure them. (What)

- Set some milestones to hit (When)

- Review the sand at the same weekly meetings where you review progress on the rock. This keeps the sand and their milestones "front of mind" for the entire company.

It's perfectly fine for a small part of the team to focus on moving the current rock while the rest of the team stays focused on pushing the sand. In this scenario, a few are entirely devoted to the rock, while the rest contribute to the rock by pushing the sand. Keep both parts informed on the progress of the other.

Another way to do this is to have everyone take part in moving the rock while at the same time continuing to push the sand.

Either way works. Picking one way or the other is related to the particular rock you are moving, the talent on your team, and the configuration of your company. Mixing it up each quarter also works well.

But whatever you do, don't stop pushing the sand.

CHAPTER 11

PICK A ROCK, MOVE IT, REPEAT

This brings us back to the beginning doesn't it? Let's review.

No matter what, your company has to keep pushing the sand, pushing more of it, and doing it better. But your company has to move rocks, while at the same time pushing the sand, or your company won't grow. And you can't move just any rocks. You have to move the right ones so that they build on each other and take your company where you want it to go.

To insure that you have selected the right rocks, you must first answer the Big Five Strategy Questions. This creates context for your selections. Then you set milestones to meet 3-5 years out, one year out and for the next 90 days.

At this point identify key thrusts, narrow them down to 3 to 5 rocks to move in the coming year and then select the right rock for the next 90 days. Finally you ask the Little Three Execution questions to make sure you move the rock. And you do the same for the sand.

Pick a rock. Move it. Repeat. Pick another rock. Move it. Repeat.

All the while, simultaneously pushing the sand.

At the most basic level, this is what strategy and execution is all about.

Good Luck.

ACKNOWLEDGEMENTS

Rock and Sand was a collaborative work born out of frustration: mine, and that of my clients.

I would work with my clients, in many different formats, to create clever, clear strategic plans. My clients bought into them and they were effective in creating direction for their organizations. Their teams bought into them as well and were generally pretty excited about them.

Still, in almost every case, execution was a problem. Teams would agree on an action to improve the company for the next ninety days, then go back to their daily routines and set the action aside. That or they tried to do too many actions at one time, making progress on none, and then default to their previous personal routines.

I was frustrated, they were frustrated.

We all liked the idea of "rocks" from *Mastering the Rockefeller Habits*, so we continued using that terminology even though we didn't really understand it. We repeatedly discussed and explored the imagery of moving rocks. I wore out numerous flip charts drawing out pictures of what we discussed. Finally one of the pictures resonated. At an executive briefing, I dropped the usual material I present and drew the latest version of the Rock and Sand drawing. It resonated unanimously among those attending, all business owners.

Not satisfied with one encounter of this type, I tried it out on numerous people, individually and in groups. I made a couple of fairly unprofessional videos of the idea and shared them.

The most common comment was, "I finally get this," followed by either a sigh of relief if they thought they were working on rocks and sand, or more likely a pained expression when they realized they weren't really moving their business forward.

I have to thank a number of people for their part in creating this idea and the subsequent video and book: Verne Harnish, who I met more than 16 years ago and without which I would never have learned that I was a talented strategy and execution guy; all of my clients over the past 12 years from In-Synk, Inner Circle, and Clarity Council, Trace Hallowell of Tactical Magic, who pushed me to frame out these ideas in a more professional manner than I would have on my own; Mark Green, Eric Mathews, Tara McAdams, and Ron Huntington, who each helped me shape the manuscript in critical ways, while always paying attention to the sensitivities of my ego.

And as always, I am thankful for the love and support of my wife and family, without which I really couldn't accomplish anything.

–Michael Synk

ABOUT THE AUTHOR

After establishing himself as a successful businessperson over a twenty-year career, Michael Synk has spent the last decade as a business educator, coach and consultant. He is one of the original sixteen coaches in North America certified by Gazelles International to teach and facilitate the highly successful Four Decisions™ curriculum which uses the One Page Strategic Plan™.

"Hard data and my own personal experience reveal that if you effectively align your strategies, actions and goals, you will be in a stronger position to leverage efficiency and growth. Everything we do is geared toward giving our executive clients the clarity they need to succeed."

Michael graduated from the University of Michigan in 1979, with a BA from the School of Education, with a Secondary School Certification in Social Studies. For two years he taught social studies as well as coached sports at Catholic High Schools in the city of Detroit.

He then embarked on business career for the next twenty years, mostly in the temporary help industry but also in health care practice management. In 2000, he started his coaching practice, In-Synk: Aligning Strategy Actions and Goals.

This is Michael's second book, the first being *How to Create Customer as Loyal as Norm Peterson, The Cheers Model of Marketing.*

Michael has been married for 26 years, has three children, and resides with his family in Memphis, Tennessee.

ABOUT ABOUT IN-SYNK

In-Synk: Aligning Strategy, Actions and Goals

In-Synk is dedicated to a simple proposition: if you effectively align your strategies, actions and goals, you will be in a stronger position to leverage efficiency and growth. Everything we do is geared toward giving our executive clients the clarity they need to succeed.

For more information go to **www.In-Synk.com**

To view the video of this concept go to **www.RocknSand.net**

To order multiple copies of *Rock and Sand: A Practical Insight to Business Growth* contact the author at:

In-Synk
1610 E. Clanlo Drive
Memphis, TN 38104

901-488-8172

msynk@in-synk.com

IN-SYNK

Aligning Strategies, Actions and Goals

IN-SYNK

Aligning Strategies, Actions and Goals

www.in-synk.com

32277058R00038

Made in the USA
Charleston, SC
14 August 2014